THE BEST OF
GOSPEL & INSPIRATIONAL
M U S I C   V O L. 1

CONTENTS

ALMIGHTY GOD

Words by
PHILL McHUGH

Music by
GREG NELSON

1. Who filled the sky with ra - diant stars
(2.) used His words to lay out _____ the foun -

Almighty God - 4 - 1

CORNERSTONE

Words and Music by
LARI GOSS

Je-sus is the Cor-ner-stone, Came for sin-ners to a-
am by sin op-pressed, On the stone I am at

tone; Tho re-ject-ed by His own He be-came the Cor-ner-
rest; When the seeds of truth are sown He re-mains the Cor-ner-

stone, Je-sus is the Cor-ner-stone. When I stone.
stone,

Rock of A-ges, cleft for

me, Let me hide my-self in Thee.

HE'S ALIVE

Words and Music by
DON FRANCISCO

gates and doors were barred_ and all _ the win - dows fast-ened down. I

spent the night_ in sleep-less-ness_ and rose at ev - ery sound.

He's Alive - 8 - 1

Half in hope-less sor-row___ and half in fear the day___ would

find the sol - diers break-in' through___ to drag us all a-

way. And

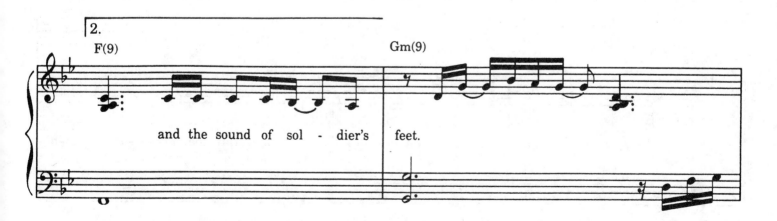

and the sound of sol - dier's feet.

12

add-ed to my shame. When at last it came to choic-es I de-nied _____ I knew His name._

And e-ven if He was_a-live it would-n't be the same._

But sud-den-ly _____ the air was filled_with a

strange and sweet per - fume. _ Light that came from ev - ery - where, drove

shad-ows from the room, _ and Je - sus stood be-fore_ me with His arms _____ held _ o-pen

16

He's Alive - 8 - 7

Verse 2:
And just before the sunrise
I heard something at the wall.
The gate began to rattle
And a voice began to call.
I hurried to the window
Looked down into the street,
Expecting swords and torches
And the sounds of soldier's feet.

SYMPHONY OF PRAISE

Words and Music by
JON MOHR and RANDALL DENNIS

Symphony Of Praise - 12 - 1

Symphony Of Praise - 12 - 3

22

praise, _____ con - duct - ed by the

An - cient _ of Days, bades cre - a - tion great or

small lift their _ voic - es one and ____ all in the sym - pho-ny _ of

praise. _____

24

Symphony Of Praise - 12 - 10

28

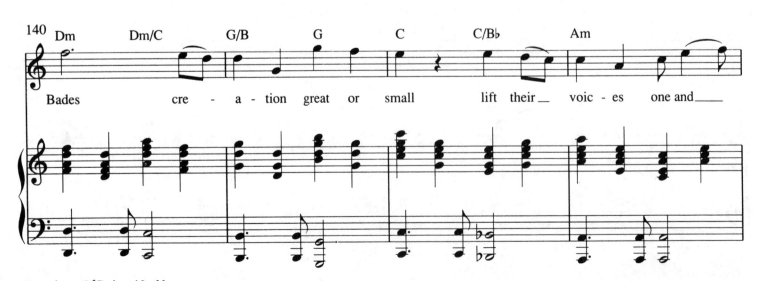

Symphony Of Praise - 12 - 11

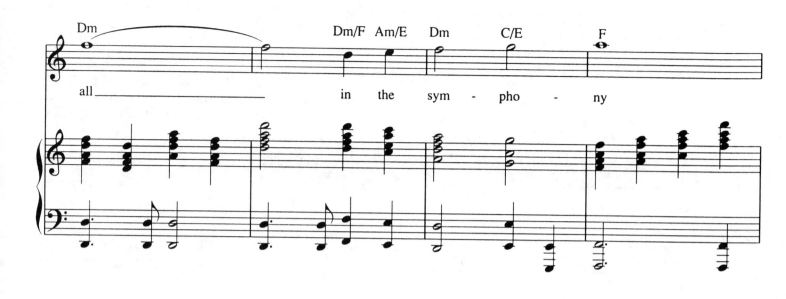

THOU ART WORTHY

Words and Music by
PAULINE MICHAEL MILLS
(Based on Revelation 4:10,11)
Arranged by FRED BOCK

Thou Art Worthy - 4 - 1

SAVED BY LOVE

Words and Music by
AMY GRANT, CHRIS SMITH
and JUSTIN PETERS

In four, with a beat ♩ = 80

1. Lau - ra loves — her lit - tle fam - 'ly, — and

Saved By Love - 7 - 1

2. There's

saved by love, ___ saved ___ by love.
(saved by ___ love, _____)

D.S. 𝄋
(to Chorus)

Coda

saved by ___ love, saved ___ by love, _____ saved ___ by ___
(saved by ___ love, _____)

Saved By Love - 7 - 6

FOOTPRINTS IN THE SAND

Moderately ♩ = 112

Words and Music by
DIANE WILLIS

Footprints In The Sand - 3 - 1

FILLED WITH JESUS

Words and Music by
DAN BURGESS

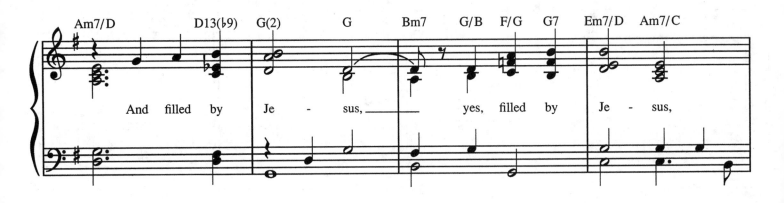

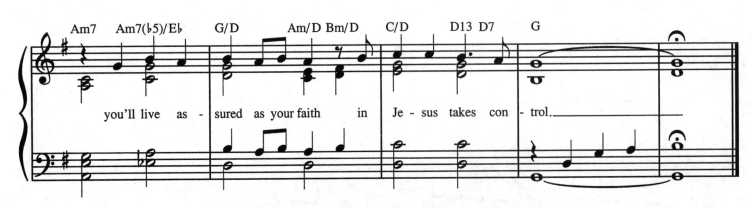

GIVE THEM ALL TO JESUS

Words and Music by
BOB BENSON, SR. and PHIL JOHNSON

Music by
PHIL JOHNSON

Give Them All To Jesus - 3 - 1

Give Them All To Jesus - 3 - 3

HE

Lyric by
RICHARD MULLAN

Music by
JACK RICHARDS

He - 2 - 1

HE'S ONLY A PRAYER AWAY

By
JOHNNY LANGE and
HAROLD L. GRAHAM

He's Only A Prayer Away - 2 - 1

CHORUS

HE'S ON-LY A PRAYER A-WAY, _____ HE'S

ON-LY A PRAYER A-WAY. _____

God will be with you when ev-er you pray. HE'S

ON-LY A PRAYER A-WAY. _____

EXTRA VERSES

— 5 —
Though you walk alone in the darkness
You're lost and there's nothin' in sight
He's with you each step of the journey
He's there with His guiding light.

— 6 —
You followed the path of a sinner
Temptation had led you astray
Remember He'll always forgive you
If you''ll only meet him halfway.

— 7 —
He has an infinite power
And so many things He can do
He'll always be ready to help you
Just ask Him to come to you.

— 8 —
Whenever you feel sad and lonely
'Cause all of your hopes fell apart
He'll bring you a new life if only
You'll keep Him within your heart.

He's Only A Prayer Away - 2 - 2

WONDERFUL NAME

Words and Music by
RODGER STRADER

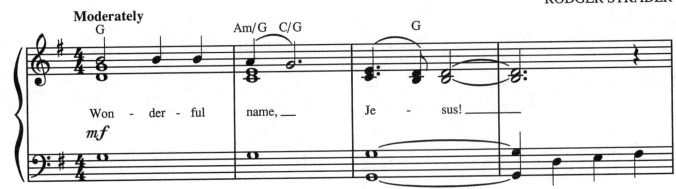

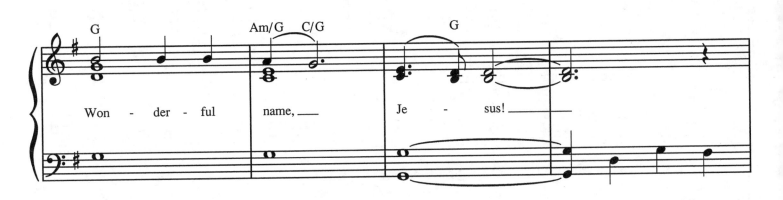

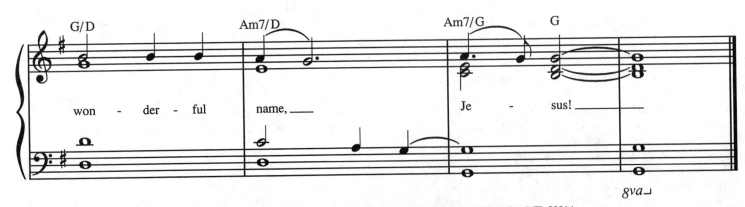

HIS KIND OF LOVE

Words and Music by
MARIJOHN WILKIN

Moderately Slow

1. "If you have seen me _____ you've seen the Fa - ther," _____ said the
2.3.(See additional lyrics)

Son. So He com - plet - ed _____ the earth - ly

task _____ He had be - gun. He let this

His Kind Of Love - 3 - 1

cost. And how the an - gels must have

cried, watch - ing help - less_____ as He died_____ to bring us

love, per - fect love,_____ His kind of

1. love.

2. Fine

D.S. al Fine

3. "It is love.

His Kind Of Love - 3 - 3

Verse 2:
I can almost feel the heavens shuddering still;
Standing helpless, watching Jesus climb that hill,
Asking help from not one man.
Perfect love makes no demands.
He walked in love, perfect love, His kind of love.
(To Chorus:)

Verse 3:
"It is finished"; those were the last words heard spoken
From the body of a man whose heart was broken.
God, condemned by man, the judge,
Accepting judgement, without one grudge,
To bring us love, perfect love, His kind of love.
(To Chorus:)

THAT GLORY BOUND TRAIN

Words and Music by
ROY ACUFF and ODELL McLEOD

That Glory Bound Train - 2 - 1

CHORUS

Has your tick-et yet been pur-chased for that GLOR-Y BOUND TRAIN? Oh will you

ride (that glor-y bound train) oh will you ride (that glor-y bound train) Will you ride that train to

glo-ry bye and bye _____ Oh the bye _____

3

When through space we will be traveling
Leavin' this wicked world of hate
Then we'll know our destination's
Just beyond those pearly gates
There we know there'll be no sorrow
As on earth we have endured
We shall dwell within His kingdom
Buy your ticket and be pure

4

When you hear it in the distant
Hear it's mighty drivers roll
Just a little while to tarry
Then we'll walk those streets of gold
Will those loved ones who have journeyed
Just a little while ago
Meet you there at Heaven's station
When that last long whistle blows

HOW GREAT THOU ART!

By
STUART K. HINE

VERSE

1. O Lord my God! When I in awe-some won-der___ Con-sid-er
2. When through the woods and for-est glades I wan-der___ And hear the
3. And when I think that God, His Son not spar-ing,___ Sent Him to
4. When Christ shall come with shout of ac-cla-ma-tion___ And take me

all the *worlds Thy hands have made,___ I see the stars, I hear the roll-ing
birds sing sweet-ly in the trees;___ When I look down from loft-y moun-tain
die, I scarce can take it in;___ That on the cross, my bur-den glad-ly
home, what joy shall fill my heart!___ Then I shall bow in hum-ble ad-o-

How Great Thou Art - 2 - 1

How Great Thou Art - 2 - 2

I AM NOT ALONE

By
JOHNNY LANGE, EVELYN MERRILL and
EDDIE BALLANTINE

When I walk thru fields of grain, God's hand is in my own. I

say a pray'r of thanks-giv-ing there, For I AM NOT A - LONE. When I

watch my chil-dren pray, With faith how strong they've grown. I

I Am Not Alone - 2 - 1

I FOUND THE ANSWER

Words and Music by
JOHNNY LANGE

1. I was weak and wea-ry, I had gone a-stray,
2. I was sad and lone-ly, All my hopes were gone,
3. Keep your Bi-ble with you, Read it ev-'ry day,

Walk-ing in the dark-ness, I could-n't find my way.
Days were long and drea-ry, I could-n't car-ry on.
Al-ways count your bless-ings and al-ways stop to pray.

Then a light came shin-ing, to lead me from des-pair,
Then I found the cou-rage to keep my head up high,
Learn to keep be-liev-ing and faith will see you through,

I Found The Answer - 2 - 1

I Found The Answer - 2 - 2

A WITCH'S INVITATION

By
CARMAN and KEITH THOMAS

A Witch's Invitation - 16 - 1

little envelope bordered with flying bats and eerie serpents whose eyes were tinted green.

The letter was addressed to me so as I opened it I froze. What I read turned my

complexion three shades of blue. It said, "My name is Isaac Horowitz. I'm a male witch, a warlock,

and I feel I need to spend some time with you." Now as a Christian

66

from a little church, with God's call on my life, a man of faith and power with a challenge to grow,

I did what any saint would do in my situation. I tore it up and said, "Lord, no way I'm gonna go."

Then gently and methodically the Holy Spirit spoke and reminded me we're God's

voice to our nation. It's the church's responsibility to witness. So, reluctantly I

accepted this witch's invitation.

mysteriously

He had the house you'd expect - the

old English cottage. A "Nightmare on Elm Street" special right to the core. The overgrown ivy,

the gate that creaked when opened; somehow you'd expect Freddy to answer this door.

A Witch's Invitation - 16 - 4

The door bell rang, a hollow gong, the knob twisted then opened and Isaac stood before me

with a grin. His jet black hair and well trimmed beard flowed with his black silk clothes.

My skin crawled as he said, "Please come on in."

His house was filled with every occultic symbol you could fathom:

you drink this stuff, next day you'll be a frog."   Then he led me to a high backed chair

as he meticulously began to unfold his scenario with evil patience.   I was given

a giant leather bound book jammed with newspaper clippings - thus the reason for this

witch's invitation.   With eagerness he pointed to each article with pride.

He said, "I healed this woman through a Babylonian chant. You see this man? I cured him while

performing druid worship. I was paid to curse this man with AIDS by his aunt."

On and on, page after page, delightfully he flaunted each incident for an hour

without a breath. He said, "Do you realize through my understanding of the dark regions that I can make

A Witch's Invitation - 16 - 8

72

you rich or even curse someone to death?"   I   sat   literally   intimidated

by   his   immensity   in   demon   power   while   his   face   shone

with   a   satanic   arrogant   bliss.   Then,   placing   his   hands   on   the   arms   of   my   chair

and   leaning   into   my   face   he   said,   "What   can   your

God do to compete with this?" I knew then

how Moses felt when he turned his rod to a serpent and the three Egyptian magicians

did the same. It's as if you're sitting there in that stunned moment while your

faith gets violated and all you feel is weak, powerless and lame.

I desperately and deeply prayed saying, "Jesus, give me wisdom-

I don't want to put You through some foolish test."

Then a shaft of light shot through my soul igniting

L.H. *mp*

my eyes with fire. God stood me up and I threw the book back in his chest. I said, "Isaac,

mf stronger

coming for you - the soft associates in your incantations - the friendly

demons you think you now control. The time will come when you'll be lying in

bed, wheezing like a dying animal, when those spirits lay claim to the rights they

own to your soul. Then the room will grow dark and the most hideous

evil faces you've ever seen will come flaming out of the floor with a yell! The vile

informants that promised reincarnation will claw your spirit and

victoriously drag your soul to hell!" Then I grabbed the book and said,

"In that moment which mantra, which incantation are you gonna chant to tell them

to leave you alone?" I said, "My friend, I know beyond a shadow of a doubt what I would say...

I am bought with the blood of Jesus. Let me go!

I said, "Isaac, when you tossed that book in my lap, you gloated with a sinister victory.

You rejoiced when you saw your name in black and white. Now I rejoice, but not that your counsel of

demons are subject to Jesus, but that my name is written in the Lamb's Book of Life!"

Then Isaac jumped up from his chair and screamed, "You must leave now!" I said,

"I will, but one last obligation - next time think twice before you rumble

with a man of God! And, by the way, thanks for your witch's invitation."

A Witch's Invitation - 16 - 16

I HAVE DECIDED TO FOLLOW JESUS

FOLK MELODY FROM INDIA

I HAVE RETURNED

Words and Music by
MARIJOHN WILKIN

I Have Returned - 3 - 1

Chorus:

turned   to the God of my   child-hood;___   Beth-le-hem's

2.3.4.(See additional lyrics)

Babe,   the proph-et's Mes- si-ah.___   He's Je-sus to me;   E-ter-nal

De-i-ty.   Praise___ His name, I have re- turned.

turned.   *molto rit.*   I have re-

turned.   *molto rit.*

To next strain slowly ad lib

Fine

Verse 2:
I have returned
To the God of my mother,
With unfailing faith
For the child of her heart.
She said bring them up
The way that you want them.
Thank God when they're grown,
They'll never depart.
(To Chorus:)

Chorus 2:
I have returned
To the God of my mother.
I learned at her knee
He's the lily of the valley.
He's Jesus to me; Eternal Deity.
Praise His name; I have returned.

Verse 3:
I have returned
To the God of my father,
The most God-like man
A child could know.
I just heard a shout
From the angels in glory,
Praising the Lord;
A child has come home.
(To Chorus:)

Chorus 3:
I have returned
To the God of my father;
Creator of heaven and earth;
God of the universe.
He's Jesus to me; Eternal Deity.
Praise His name; I have returned.

Chorus 4:
I have returned
To the Father of Abraham,
The shepherd of Moses
Who called Him the great I am.
He's Jesus to me; Eternal Deity.
Praise His name; I have returned.

I Have Returned - 3 - 3

THERE IS PEACE

Words and Music by
RODGER STRADER

Chorus:

peace _____ there is peace, _____ in the

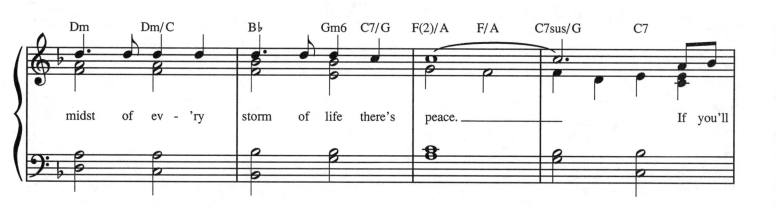

midst of ev - 'ry storm of life there's peace. _____ If you'll

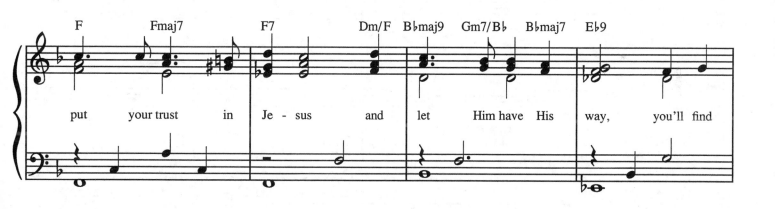

put your trust in Je - sus and let Him have His way, you'll find

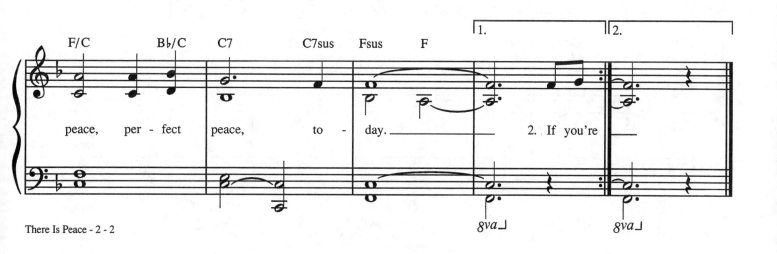

peace, per - fect peace, to - day. _____ 2. If you're

I SAW THE LIGHT

Words and Music by
HANK WILLIAMS

INTRO.

VERSE

1. I wan-dered so aim-less___ life filled with sin.
2. Just like a blind man I wan-dered a-long.
3. I was a fool to___ wan-der and stray.

I would-n't let my dear Sav-iour in.___
Wor-ries and fears I claimed for my own.___
Straight is the gate and nar-row the way.___

Then Je-sus came like a stran-ger in the night
Then like the blind man that God gave back his sight
Now I have trad-ed the wrong___ for the right

I Saw The Light - 2 - 1

Praise the Lord _____ I SAW THE LIGHT.
Praise the Lord _____ I SAW THE LIGHT.
Praise the Lord _____ I SAW THE LIGHT.

CHORUS G

I SAW THE LIGHT ___ I SAW THE LIGHT ___ No more dark - ness,

C

G

No more night ___ Now I'm so hap - py, no sor - row in sight. ___

1. D7 G

2. D7 G

Praise the Lord ___ I SAW THE LIGHT.   I SAW THE LIGHT.

I Saw The Light - 2 - 2

IF I CAN GIVE

By
JOHNNY LANGE and **TONY FONTANE**
(ASCAP)

If I Can Give - 3 - 1

can, _____ So I can help _____ my fel-low man, I on-ly want _____ to do my part _____ to lift a tired _____ or wear-y heart. To guide a soul _____ who lost his way _____ to help him see _____ a bright-er day, To let him know _____ I un-der-

If I Can Give - 3 - 2

SWEET, SWEET SPIRIT

Words and Music by
DORIS AKERS

Sweet, Sweet Spirit - 3 - 1

Sweet, Sweet Spirit - 3 - 3

IN GETHSEMANE ALONE

Words and Music by
MARIJOHN WILKIN

In Gethsemane Alone - 4 - 1

2. Forgive me if you sometimes see me cry,
    But at times there's none more lonesome Lord than I;
    And the human hurt I'm going through,
    Dear Lord, I know you have felt it too.
    And you won't leave me in Gethsemane alone. *(Chorus:)*

3. While the whole world slept He kept watch alone,
    Knowing with the morning He'd be gone;
    And the human hurt we put Him through,
    Only God and the angels knew;
    In Gethsemane, in Gethsemane alone. *(Chorus:)*

THERE'S SOMEONE TO HELP YOU

By
JOHNNY LANGE
(ASCAP)

There's Someone To Help You - 2 - 1

There's Someone To Help You - 2 - 2

IT IS WELL WITH MY SOUL

HORATIO G. SPAFFORD

PHILIP P. BLISS

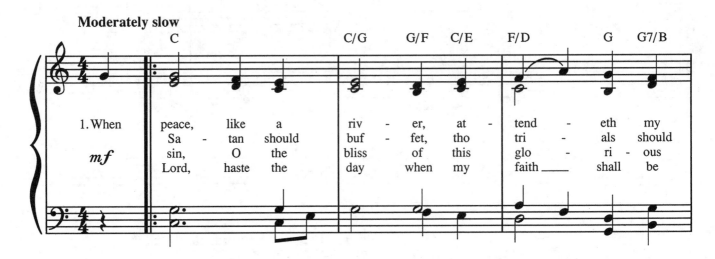

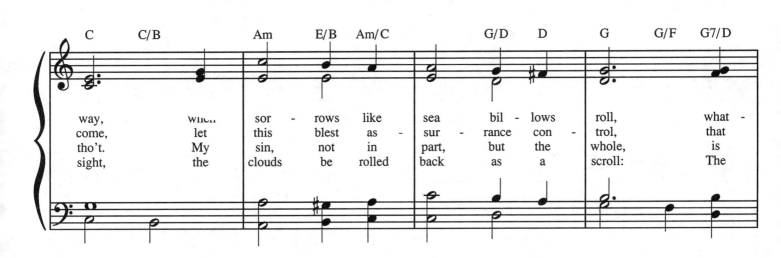

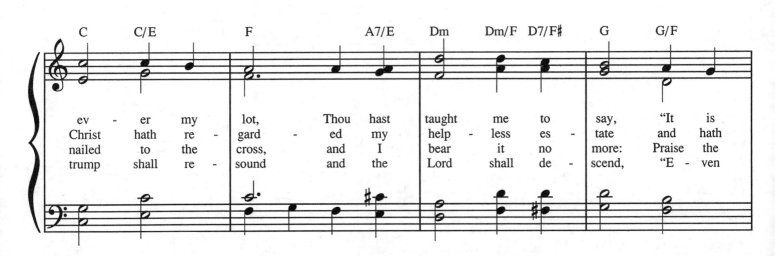

It Is Well with My Soul - 2 - 1

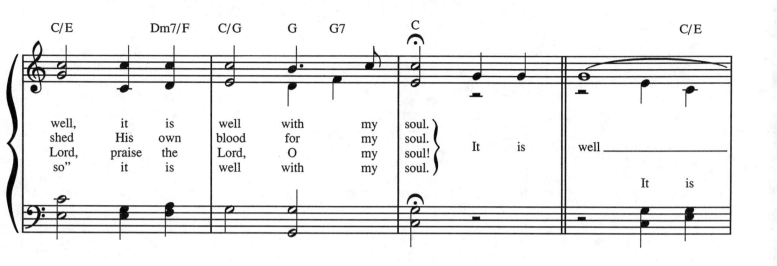

IN THIS QUIET TIME OF PRAYER

Words and Music by
DAVID JUSTICE

IT WASN'T HIS CHILD

Words and Music by
SKIP EWING

It Wasn't His Child - 5 - 1

Bridge:

It Wasn't His Child - 5 - 2

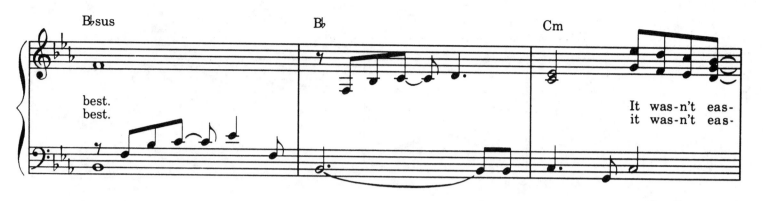

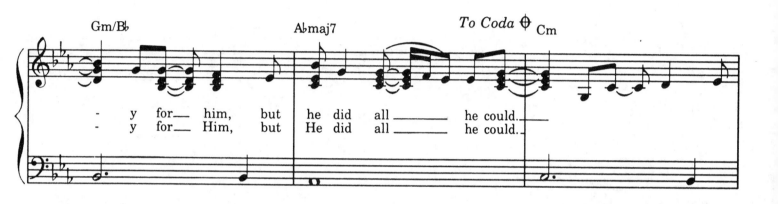

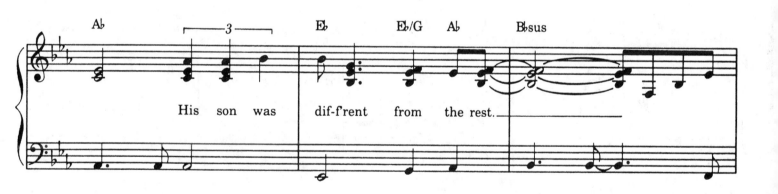

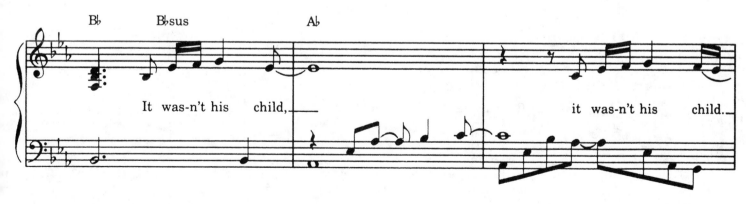

It Wasn't His Child - 5 - 3

Coda

He grew up with His hands__ in wood, and He

died with His hands__ in wood. He was God's__ child.__

He was God's__ child.__

He was her man, she was his

wife. And late one win - ter night, he knelt by her as she

gave birth. But it was-n't his child.

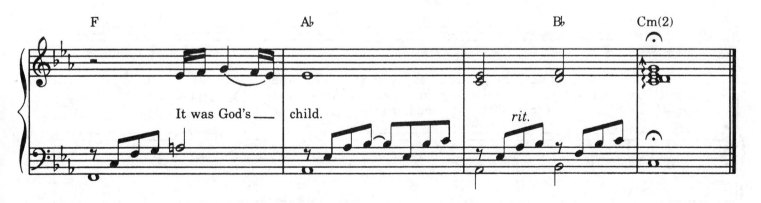

It was God's child.

It Wasn't His Child - 5 - 5

(Put Your Heart in the Bible)

KEEP THE BIBLE IN YOUR HEART

By
JOHNNY LANGE and HY HEATH
(ASCAP)

Keep The Bible In Your Heart - 2 - 1

Then
When you're liv-ing like the Bi-ble tells you to.
Then

CHORUS

Put your heart in _____ the Bi - ble, _____ KEEP THE BI - BLE IN YOUR

HEART. ____ (1. 2.) If you want to find ____ real peace of mind ____ KEEP THE
(3) Read it ev - 'ry day ____ and when you pray ____

BI - BLE IN YOUR HEART.   2. Now, HEART. ____
                                  3. If

LET YOUR LOVE FLOW THROUGH ME

RODGER STRADER

Let Your Love Flow Through Me - 2 - 1

Let Your Love Flow Through Me - 2 - 2

MAKING WAR IN THE HEAVENLIES

Words and Music by
GEORGE SEARCY

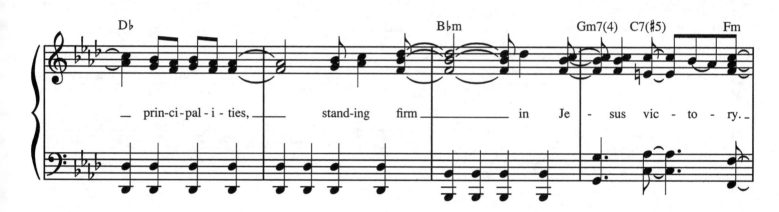

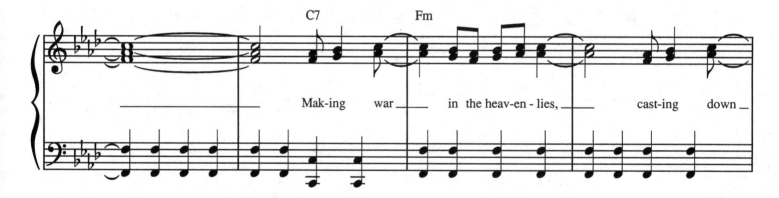

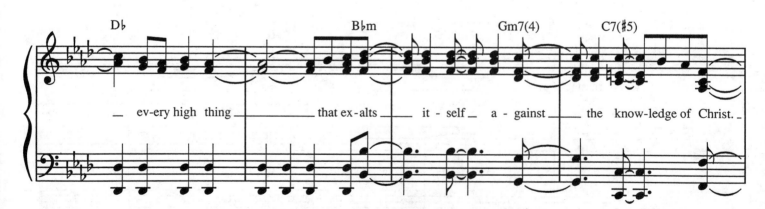

Making War in the Heavenlies - 2 - 1

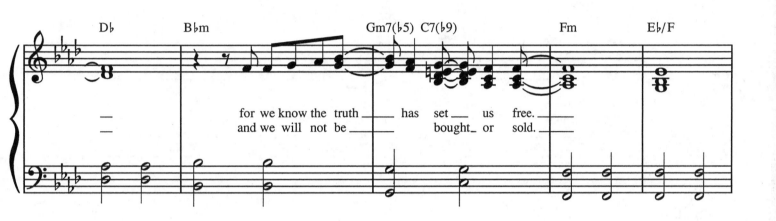

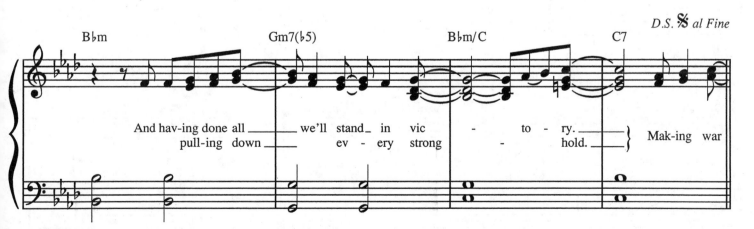

Making War in the Heavenlies - 2 - 2

THE MIGHTY HILLS OF GOD

Words and Music by
MARIJOHN WILKIN

The Mighty Hills Of God - 2 - 1

TOGETHER

RODGER STRADER
Arranged by BOB KROGSTAD

Organ: Ped.

1. Be-fore the world be -

gan, _____ Our un-ion was His plan, _____
day, _____ Our God we will o - bey, _____

Together - 4 - 1

Our lone-ly days are gone, _____ To-geth-er we'll be
And He will lead us from _____ The trou-bled times that

one; _____ Wher - ev - er you may go, _____
come; _____ And with your hand in mine, _____

Wher - ev - er you may lodge, _____ What - ev - er you will
We'll stand the test of time, _____ And through the dark-est

do, _____ I will be with you. _____
night, _____ The Lord will be our light. _____ And we'll go

Together - 4 - 3

lives in - to His hands of love.

With-in our home this

Yield - ing our lives in - to His hands of

love.

Together - 4 - 4

RADIO STATION S-A-V-E-D

Words and Music by
ROY ACUFF and ODELL McLEOD

Oh they say there'll be a judg'ment, That it may come an-y day Will you be prepared for
You get news di-rect from hea-ven From that glo-ry-land on high Where there is no in-ter-
Each and ev-'ry one are welcome To the stu-di-os of Christ There'll be Angels there to

Je-sus, has He brightened up your way He will take the torch of glo-ry as the
fer-ence or no sta-tic in the sky All the programs are of hap-pi-ness and
greet you Oh they'll treat you ve-ry nice Here they do not charge ad-mis-sion, It is

Bi-ble it did say It's the mi-chro-phone of Je-sus o-ver S-A-V-E-D.
nev-er no dis-pair It's the on-ly radi-o sta-tion that is nev-er off the air.
free to one and all. Won't you get in tune with Je-sus, please do not neg-lect His call.

Radio Station S - A - V - E - D - 2 - 1

CHORUS

Oh this sta-tion's owned and op-er-at-ed By the soul of Je-sus.

Won't you lis-ten in to sta-tion S - A - V - E - D, If the

road is dark and storm-y And you can-not see your way Why not

turn your dial to Je-sus, Won't you lis-ten in to - day. 2.You get day. 3. Each and

rit.

NO OTHER LIKE YOU

Words and Music by
PAULA CARPENTER and MARK COMDEN

1. Love, like the end - less sky___ that al - ways cov - ers me,___ Ex - ten - ing up___ so high
2. Peace, like a gen - tle stream___ flows to ev - 'ry part,___ It wash - es o - ver me,
3. Hope, like a burn - ing flame___ glow-ing deep___ with - in___ When noth - ing stays___ the same

No Other Like You - 4 - 2

No Other Like You - 4 - 3

No Other Like You - 4 - 4

O PERFECT LOVE

Words and Music by
JOSEPH BARNBY

O Perfect Love - 2 - 1

O Perfect Love - 2 - 2

SOMEBODY BIGGER THAN YOU AND I

Words and Music by
JOHNNY LANGE, HY HEATH
and SONNY BURKE

Moderato (with much feeling)

Chorus

Who made the moun-tain, who made the tree, Who made the riv-er flow to the sea, And who hung the moon in the star-ry sky? SOME-BOD-Y BIG-GER THAN YOU AND I.

Who makes the flow-ers bloom in the spring, Who writes the song for the rob-in to sing, And who sends the rain when the earth is dry? SOME-BOD-Y BIG-GER THAN

Somebody Bigger Than You And I - 2 - 1

THE OLD RUGGED CROSS

Words by GEORGE BENNARD
Based on 1 Cor. 1:22-25

Music by
GEORGE BENNARD

Refrain:

cher - ish the old rug - ged cross, _____ till my
cross the old rug - ged cross,

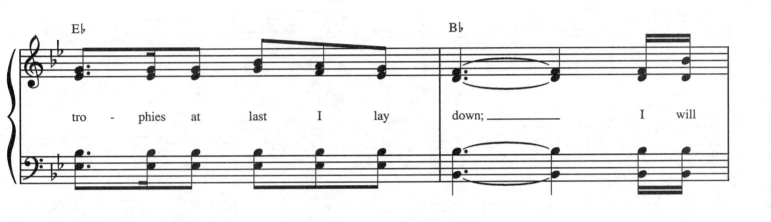

tro - phies at last I lay down; _____ I will

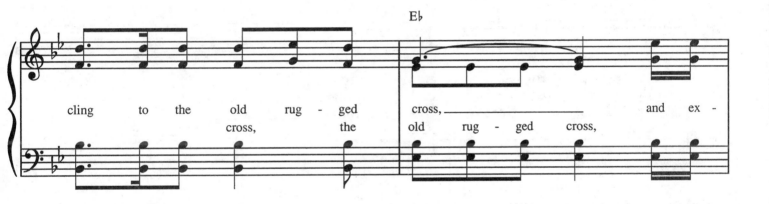

cling to the old rug - ged cross, _____ and ex -
cross, the old rug - ged cross,

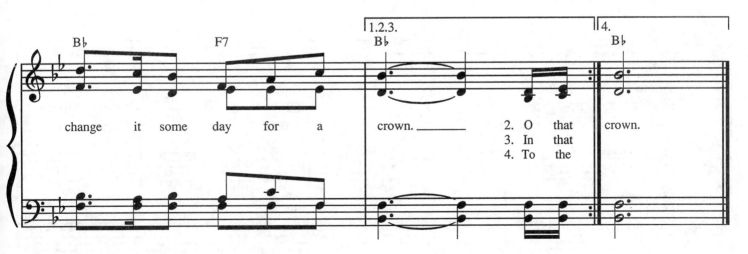

change it some day for a crown. _____
2. O that crown.
3. In that
4. To the

The Old Rugged Cross - 2 - 2

PASS IT ON

Words and Music by
KURT KAISER

MY TASK

Words by
MAUDE LOUISE RAY

Music by
E.L. ASHFORD

love some-one more dear-ly ev-ery day, ____ to help a wan-d'ring child to find his way ____
fol-low truth, for-ev-er seek-ing light, ____ to do my best from dawn un-til the night, ____

to pon-der o'er a no-ble thought and pray, ____ and smile when eve-ning falls, ___ and smile when eve-ning falls, this is my task.
to keep my heart fit for His ho-ly sight, ____ and an-swer when he calls, ___ and an-swer when he calls,

1.

2.
this is my task, this is my task.

PRESS ON

DAN BURGESS

When the val - ley is deep, when the moun - tain is steep, When the bod - y is wea - ry, when we stum - ble and fall; ____

RISE AGAIN

Words and Music by
DALLAS HOLM

Moderately Slow

1. Go a - head, Drive the nails ___ in my hands; ___ Laugh at me where you stand; ___ Go a - head, and say it is - n't me; The

day ___ will come ___ when you ___ will see! ___ 'Cause I'll

CHORUS:

(1 - 2) rise ___ a - gain; Ain't no pow'r on ___
(3) come ___ a - gain; Ain't no pow'r on ___

earth can tie ___ me down; ___ Yes, I'll rise ___ a -
earth can keep ___ me back; ___ Yes, I'll come ___ a -

gain; Death can't keep me ___ in the ground! ___ 2. Go a -
gain; Come to take my ___ peo - ple back. ___

3rd X to

Rise Again - 4 - 2

WHEN I MADE MY DECISION

Words and Music by
JOHNNY LANGE

Moderato with feeling

VERSE

1. I was a lost sin - ner, ____ I was a lost stray, ____ A-lone in the
(2.) The fears that have chained me, ____ I've cast them a - way, ____ No more I am
(3.) Of wrongs I've been guil - ty, ____ I've learned to un do, ____ And those who have

dark - ness ____ and wea - ry of sin; ____ I called to my Sa - vior ___
bur - dened ____ with sor - row and pain; ____ My cup of con - tent - ment __
wronged me ____ I've learned to for - give; ____ Through faith and be - liev - ing __

__ to show me the way, ____ His arms were wide o - pen __ and He took me in. ___
__ is filled ev -'ry day, ____ It's a won - der - ful feel - ing __ to be liv-ing a - gain.
__ I'm liv - ing a - new, ____ I'll be prais-ing my Sa - vior __ as long as I live. ___

When I Made My Decision - 2 - 1

4. The Lord is my Shepherd - To Him I belong,
I follow Him closely - For He is my Guide;
With Him I have courage - For He makes me strong,
The power of Jesus - Cannot be denied. (Chorus)

5. My troubles and sorrow - He shared from the start;
And all through the darkness - He walked by my side;
The Spirit of Jesus - Is here in my heart,
He's living within me - And I'm satisfied. (Chorus)

TODAY

Words and Music by
RANDY SPARKS

Moderately slow

WHY HAVE YOU CHOSEN ME?

Words and Music by
RODGER STRADER
Arranged by BOB KROGSTAD

1. Why have You cho-sen me out of mil-lions Your child to be? You
know all the wrong that I've done; O how could You par-don me, for-give my in-iq-ui-ty To

2. I am a-mazed to know that a God so great could love me so, Is
will-ing and want-ing to bless; His grace is so won-der-ful, His mer-cy so boun-ti-ful— I

Why Have You Chosen Me? - 3 - 1

CHORUS

Why Have You Chosen Me? - 3 - 2

Why Have You Chosen Me? - 3 - 3

MY TRIBUTE
(To God Be the Glory)

A.C.

Words and Music by
ANDRAÉ CROUCH

152

My Tribute - 3 - 3